The
SECRET
of
THINK
and
GROW
RICH

The
SECRET
of
THINK
and
GROW
RICH

The Inner Dimensions
of the Greatest Success
Program of All Time

MITCH HOROWITZ
Author of *The Miracle Club*

Published 2019 by Gildan Media LLC
aka G&D Media
www.GandDmedia.com

FIRST EDITION 2019

Interior design by Meghan Day Healey of Story Horse, LLC

Library of Congress Cataloging-in-Publication Data is available upon request

ISBN: 978-1-7225-0223-2

10 9 8 7 6 5 4 3 2 1

Contents

Author's Note

This short book is adapted from a talk I delivered in the spring of 2019. It captures not only what I consider the "secret" of *Think and Grow Rich* but also explores four steps at the heart of Napoleon Hill's program, including the intriguing and important question of "sex transmutation." In this book I provide personal details from my own life that highlight how best to engage in and benefit from Hill's insights. I hope you will find this a powerful introduction to *Think and Grow Rich*—and, if you're a veteran reader, I believe that what you find here will be the turn key that opens the book's most valuable insights to you. Everything in these pages is based on my direct experience. At the end of this book you will also find my condensation of *Think and Grow Rich*. This is not a substitute for the original but is useful as a refresher or source of review. The condensation contains all of Napoleon Hill's core points that appear in the original.

Introduction

To Those Who Are Ready

I consider readers and listeners of this short book part of a community of the search. It's very meaningful for me to be able communicate with you in this way, because every time I talk or write about the ideas of Napoleon Hill I inevitably learn new things myself. I arrive at fresh emphases and insights. When I find myself writing and speaking to a group of like-minded seekers, I make connections that would otherwise never occur.

This little volume is very special to me because it deals with the inner workings of a program that has literally been life changing for me, which is *Think and Grow Rich*. There is so much that I could say about Hill's 1937 program—indeed, I am currently writing a ten-book series on it. *The Secret of*

Think and Grow Rich is not intended as a blow-by-blow run through of everything that appears in Hill's table of contents. For that, my hope and my wish is that you've already read *Think and Grow Rich*, or that you will read it, and that you will read it multiple times.

What I intend here is to describe exactly the inner reason why *Think and Grow Rich* is so effective, how the author Napoleon Hill put it together, and its four most powerful, applicable points. If you apply these four points to your life, you will experience dramatic, positive change. That is a personal promise from the perspective of my own lived experience.

In *Think and Grow Rich*, Hill promises that a great "secret" to success is encoded throughout the book, and that this secret appears at least once in every chapter. "The secret to which I refer," he wrote, "has been mentioned no fewer than a hundred times throughout this book. It has not been directly named, for it seems to work more successfully when it is merely uncovered and left in sight, where THOSE WHO ARE READY, and SEARCHING FOR IT, may pick it up . . . If you are READY to put it to use, you will recognize this secret at least once in every chapter."

Although Hill's secret can be stated in words—and I will shortly do so—he also noted that this secret would never disclose itself to you in practical ways without certain self-insights and personal actions. That is what the rest of this program is dedicated to.

Chapter 1

Reading *Think and Grow Rich* in a Certain Way

I want to address you in a very personal manner in this book. I am so filled with exuberance about *Think and Grow Rich* that I almost border on the evangelical when I talk about it, and I want to justify that to you.

I knew about *Think and Grow Rich* for many years before I understood its real power. The book was on the periphery of my vision for a long time. Up until fall 2018, I had worked in book publishing for close to three decades. For part of that time—about ten years—I was the editor-in-chief of a metaphysical, body-mind-spirit imprint at Penguin, called Tarcher. In 2005, a colleague and I reissued *Think and Grow Rich* with some updates. We did it almost on a lark, but much to our surprise, the new edition dramatically took off. In many respects, it saved the imprint. Thanks to the success of that book, during the Great Recession of 2008, which our country has never really come to terms with and which we're still feeling reverberations from, no one from my imprint was laid off. I'm very proud of that. That's one of the signal accomplishments of my tenure there. To a very great degree the imprint's financial health rested on our modest reissue of *Think and Grow Rich*, a book that is in public domain in its earliest edition but that nonetheless sold about one million copies for us.

So, I had a great deal of love for the book and awareness of the book, but I must also confess that my own immersion in it at that time was tangential. I did what many readers do: I picked around in it, read around in it, and I drew the hasty conclusion that I was familiar with some of its ideas. I thought: "Well, I'm already a veteran when it comes to self-help and motivational philosophy, and some of these steps are too basic for me; I've already done some of these things as part of different programs. So I can pick my shots."

Thinking that way, I never derived any seismic benefit from the book. But later I faced a crisis in life. In the year 2013 I wasn't sure what my future was; I wasn't sure about my job security. I knew that I wanted to dedicate myself to writing, speaking, and presenting full time—which I do today—but I was burdened with uncertainty. So, I made the decision in fall 2013 to sit down and read *Think and Grow Rich* not in some casual way—not skimming or cherry picking ideas from it—but I determined to read it through and act on it as though my life depended on it. I committed to do every single exercise in the book without fail, without reservation, and with nothing but total, passionate commitment.

I must tell you that things in my life began to change dramatically for the better. Career opportunities opened to me. Writing opportunities and contracts came my way. Substantial sums of money came my way. Myriad opportunities arose to narrate books, write books, and write articles for national audiences. Television-hosting opportunities arrived. Various forms of speaking and voice-over work came to me. I had already been on that trajectory, but my dedication to *Think and Grow Rich*—treating it like urgently needed operating instructions for life—made a huge and still-unfolding difference in the momentum of everything that was occurring.

To this day, whenever a friend, family member, or someone I care about tells me that his or her life is stuck, that they're depressed or anxious or they feel like everything they've worked for is stalled or coming to nothing, I tell them: "I'll make a deal with you. I will give you a copy of *Think and Grow Rich* and work with you on it, but you must read it and do all its steps as though your life depends on it." When I tell them that I'm not trying to be morbid; it's simply that the book will disclose its efficacy in no other way. There are no halfway measures with this book. And there are none in life. *Think and Grow Rich* delivers you only if you approach it with absolute, passionate resolve. That's part of its secret.

Forgive the repetition, but I emphasize this only because I mean it so deeply: *you must approach the book and do its exercises as if your life depends on it.* And, once again, I promise you, seeker to seeker, *things will happen.* Good things will enter your life. It has happened to me. I've watched it happen to others. I'm profoundly touched by stories that I hear from people from varying walks of life who tell me things like: "My life was a total wreck, and I sat in my house for five days and I read *Think and Grow Rich*; I did everything that the book said and I found my path." This can be your experience too.

Chapter 2

The Birth of an Idea

Where did *Think and Grow Rich* come from? I want to say a quick word about that before I get into its most potent, actionable steps—and its secret.

The book appeared in 1937 from Napoleon Hill, a motivational writer and journalist who was born in Virginia. Hill had bopped around in various jobs but said that in 1908 he had a defining, life-changing experience. As a young business journalist Hill landed the ultimate "get"—an interview with world-famous steel magnate Andrew Carnegie. Carnegie, so Hill reported, told the young journalist that he should make a comprehensive study of whether a set of common traits appear in the lives of high-achievers across a wide range of fields, including diplomats, inventors, generals, politicians, and entrepreneurs. Carnegie said that anyone who has attained remarkable distinction should be studied, and their experience assembled into a comparative catalogue to determine whether there existed common principles of success.

Some have questioned whether this meeting really occurred. Andrew Carnegie died in 1919, and he wasn't around to back up or contradict Hill's story about their encounter, which Hill began describing in 1928. Carnegie did write his own autobiography, which appeared in 1920, but he made no mention of having met the fetching young journalist. Nor did Hill publish an article contemporaneous to his reported interview. But Hill's story is not implausible, either. It is a fact that in 1908 Hill was a journalist writing for a general interest and inspirational monthly called *Bob Taylor's Magazine*. The publisher Bob Taylor had been the governor of Tennessee, and later bankrolled his own magazine. (It wasn't unusual then that publishers would put their own name in front of a magazine. Some still exist today: *Harper's* in the U.S. and *Maclean's* in Canada.)

Bob Taylor's Magazine was a densely packed and lavishly illustrated journal that featured profiles of American industrialists and articles about different regions of the country and their economic and cultural traits. The magazine ran detailed articles about engineering marvels like the great dams, the new skyscrapers, and the laying of railroad tracks. I have an author photo of Napoleon Hill at age twenty-five that appeared in the magazine with his byline the year he described meeting Carnegie. It wouldn't be unusual for a journalist from *Bob Taylor's Magazine* to land an interview with someone like Carnegie, maybe with Taylor's help, and write the type of profile that was then in vogue of how an industrialist had risen in life. The robber barons, industrialists, and steel magnates loved telling stories—apocryphal or not—about how they overcame adversity and poverty to bound up the ladder of success. So, there's nothing unusual about Hill's claim—yet no such article ever appeared from his pen, and Carnegie died without weighing in.

Nonetheless, it is a fact that Hill embarked on a study, of about twenty years, looking into the question that he said Carnegie put to him of whether you can discern common traits in the lives of highly successful people. That research translated into Hill's first book, a massive and deeply interesting multi-volume study published in 1928 called *The Law of Success*. It's an outstanding book on human nature, and I highly recommend it. I've studied it carefully. It is filled with insights and serviceable ideas. Hill, to a very great extent, spent the remainder of his career, which ran until his death in 1970, reprocessing or digesting this basic set of ideas.

His most successful re-processing was in the form of *Think and Grow Rich* in 1937. *Think and Grow Rich* is, to a very great extent, a refinement of ideas that were explored at greater length, sometimes with less elegance, in *The Law of Success*. Hill brought to his new book one of the greatest consumer titles ever. Who among us wouldn't want to know how to think and grow rich? Of course, for some people today the title seems gauche or they're put off by what they consider a surface tone of materialism or selfishness. I used to be one such person. It's probably why I didn't more fully attach myself to *Think and Grow Rich* until later in life. But if you can get past the embarrassment of reading a book that might sound, on its surface, a little selfish, a little fantastical, or even a little unserious—and I can assure you it is none of those things—you stand to discover the greatest modern program on how to concretize your ideas into reality.

This is true whatever the nature of your goal. Of course, your goal may be money making. Hill geared the book in that direction. This was a time when America was still finding its way out of the Great Depression. At that time in particular, but really any time in American life, people are concerned, for very valid reasons, about money getting. Hill was also a great communicator, and he knew a great title. *Think and Grow Rich* was more than a good title; it was epic. But rest assured— the book's program and ideas can be applied in the direction of any ethical aim. I often tell people from various walks of life—artists, soldiers, students, activists—if you're not reading *Think and Grow Rich*, you're selling yourself short.

Chapter 3

What Is the Secret?

I've already said that I encourage you to read and reread *Think and Grow Rich* many times. My most cherished copy of *Think and Grow Rich* is covered in clear packing tape because I have read it so often that it would fall apart if I didn't protect it. My edition is filled with notes and observations. I've underlined and highlighted many passages. I once found in my original edition a mysterious yellow sticky note, which I will soon tell you about. I'm glad I still have this little sticky note; it marked another turning point in my life in connection with the book.

In short, *Think and Grow Rich* is a tactile, working experience. It must be read with pen in hand. And, as I've already noted, everything in it must be done.

Napoleon Hill says early in the book, and repeats at several junctures, that there's a secret in its pages. But he won't spell out the secret for you because you will benefit more if you arrive at it from your own devices. Well, I'm going to tell you what the secret is. I've found it, and I want to share it with you. The reason I'm going to share it is not because I am disregarding Hill's instructions but rather because I believe that if you've read his book carefully or plan to you will discover the same secret for yourself, and I want to help you pinpoint and apply it; and if you haven't read it carefully, or do not plan to, one or more indirect restatements of the secret will make no difference. I also believe that at this point, with the book more than eighty years old, I can talk plainly about this topic.

The secret of *Think and Grow Rich* to which Napoleon Hill refers, and which he says is encrypted throughout the book, is the following. These are my words, but they're faithful to the book:

> *Emotionalized thought directed toward one passionately held aim, aided by organized planning and the Master Mind, is the root of all accomplishment.*

I will repeat that:

Emotionalized thought directed toward one passionately held aim, aided by organized planning and the Master Mind, is the root of all accomplishment.

The most important words in that statement are: *passionately held aim.* I cannot overstate the foundational importance of possessing a definite chief aim. That is at the heart of *Think and Grow Rich.* It is the skeleton key to the rest of the program. If you have an exclusive, obsessive, passionately felt aim, everything becomes open to you. Without that, nothing will open to you, nothing will disclose itself. This is the first of four steps I will review.

I've written an entire book on this subject, it's called *The Miracle of a Definite Chief Aim.* I often say to people when I'm speaking in terms of practical philosophy that if you take just one idea from my work, make it this: You must have one passionately, obsessively held aim in life. It's the doorway to everything else. It's a natural law that concentration of energies brings force. This is true of concentrated air, water, and light—photons densely concentrated into a beam become a lascr. It's a natural law that force comes from concentration. The same is true with our psychological and psychical energies. You'll find this point in every piece of wisdom literature from the Tao Te Ching to Ralph Waldo Emerson. Concentration is power.

You must search for your personal aim in a way that permits no hiding, no internal dishonesty, no self-delusion, no peer pressure, no subterfuge, and no rote or habitual thought. You withdraw to the intimate recesses of your psyche and ask yourself in a completely unembarrassed, and unconditioned way: What do I want from life? What do I *really* want? Ask this in a plain and profoundly honestly manner.

So, again: What is your aim? It cannot be general. It cannot be vague. It can't involve a diffusion of different purposes and energies, like traveling to exotic places while also raising a young family.

Your aim must be actionable. That is a mark of an authentic aim. Otherwise it's a daydream or escapism. What if I told you, "I'd like to be on the Olympic swimming team." Well, as of this writing, I'm 53 years old. That aim is not realistic. I cannot take meaningful steps in that direction. That's a pipedream. However, if it is possible to take even small steps in the direction of your aim, then it's authentic. In this sense, you must ask: Have I got the training for what I want to do, or can I acquire it? Am I in the right place geographically? The

answer may be that you don't have certain prelim-
inary skills or abilities, but that you may be able to
come into them.

I have used the term "obsessive" to describe a
true aim. We think of an obsession as being negative. We see an obsession as a pathology, which
needs to be diagnosed and treated. But I must tell
you, seeker to seeker, that most of the people you
admire in life, most of your heroes, did possess
an obsessive aim, something they pursued with
almost exclusive intensity.

For Nelson Mandela, it was the principle of
individual dignity and democracy. For Steve
Jobs, it was the creation of a wireless, portable,
digital technology. For Thomas Jefferson, it was
the establishment of a republic that protected
the individual search for meaning. For Freder-
ick Douglass, it was ending slavery. I could name
hundreds more, ranging from soldiers and diplomats to activists and artists. In general, we know
relatively little about the lives of many of these
people. I don't know what kind of sibling Helen
Keller was. I know that she stood for and extolled
the principle of human potential. For Andrew
Carnegie, his passion was the making and market-
ing of steel. It doesn't sound very romantic, but it
did allow him to fund a network of museums and
universities all over the country.

People of exceptional achievement usually possess one absolute, defining aim. Their aim is exquisitely clear and plain. It is so plain that it can be reduced to a single sentence. And you must be able to do this with your own aim.

Having an absolute focus is at the heart of a transcendent but tough bargain that life offers us, which is this: You will receive exactly what you want, or something close to it, provided you make it your exclusive focus. And that can be a tough bargain because, as I am very aware, life places multiple demands on us. We're parents, care-givers, workers, artists, breadwinners, and so on. We face all kinds of demands. This is all the more reason to choose your aim carefully, because one well-selected aim can cover a lot of bases.

But I must be frank: your aim may not cover *all* the bases. But it will be yours and it will be pas-sionate. And this is profoundly important because we communicate with the subconscious, with our psychical and interior selves, through the emotions. Exuberance, enthusiasm, persistence—these are emotionally driven states of being. And entering these states is the only way that you actu-ally get anything done.

On a personal level, people often ask me: "You seem to get so much done, don't you ever get any sleep? How is it that you have such boundless enthusiasm?" Well I do sleep, but I'm so driven by the passion of my aim—which is documenting metaphysical experience in history and practice—that I want it more than I want to eat, more than I want to sleep, more than I want to crack open a beer. In fact, at this point in my life, I'm largely sober, because I want to have all my energy at the ready to dedicate to my work. And, anybody who knows me, whether intimately or as a reader or co-seeker, knows how passionate I am about my writing, speaking, and narrating. It drives me—it fills me with passion. When you possess a definite chief aim of the type that I'm talking about, you will discover energies in yourself that you never knew existed. Whenever I talk about *Think and Grow Rich,* I spend more time on this topic than any other, because it is the skeleton key to all the rest.

Chapter 4

The Dynamism of Organized Planning

You must exercise organized planning in pursuit of your aim. Organized planning is step two. As I noted earlier: Emotionalized thought directed toward one passionately held aim, aided by *organized planning* and the Master Mind, is the root of all accomplishment. There is *doing* involved in this. Again, an aim, to be authentic, must be actionable. You must be able to take concrete steps in the direction of what you wish to be doing.

Your wish cannot be a pipedream but it can still be very bold. I was in contact with a man who held a good job in a real estate agency in Washington D.C.; he was in his late thirties and he said he wanted to be a film producer. He wondered: "Is this just too far out?" I told him, so long as you can take reasonable steps in the direction of your wish, it's not too far out. And I began to communicate with him about things that he could do: there are lots of colleges and universities around D.C. There are lots of artists in and around D.C. He should attend film festivals and focus on short films and documentaries. Find out what local filmmakers are doing. See if he could help them with treatments and with funding. Maybe he can provide micro-funding in certain cases. Maybe he can help certain documentaries get exposed to other producers, foundations, or investors who can provide backing. Maybe he assists indie filmmakers with treatments and business opportunities—that's what producers do. There exist so many opportunities for exposure. Such opportunities are not always money making, but for documentarians and makers of short films and student film projects, festivals and viewings are the seedlings of other things that are much bigger. Help artists find their way to such venues, I counseled him. And further, know everything there is to know about what young filmmakers and independent filmmakers and artists deal with in the marketplace today. You can start right in D.C. You're not on the planet Mars. You're in a metropolitan area that has lots of schools and artists. Take these steps and effectively you are functioning as a producer.

I was trying to get across to my correspondent that if film producing is really your passionate aim, and it is something you want as dearly as drawing breath, there *are* concrete steps that can be taken in that direction. It may not be remunerative at first—or not at all. There are lots of artists and entrepreneurs who keep day jobs. I kept a day job, in effect, for many years. You cannot immediately or always wed your dream to paying the rent. But, nonetheless, movement is possible. Now, if the man had told me that he wanted to be the first astronaut to go to Mars, I'd have dismissed that. You'd have to do a lot of convincing to demonstrate that you could do something on Tuesday that would help further that aim. But I can be convinced, and he could be convinced, that he *could* do something on Tuesday that would further him in becoming a film producer.

This program is not one of passivity. This is not a program of sitting back and hoping things will happen to you. Indeed, I can instantly tell when somebody hasn't read *Think and Grow Rich* because they caricature it as a program of passivity or magical thinking. In the same way that your seventh-grade English teacher could immediately tell whether you read *Lord of the Flies* or *A Separate Peace* or *Animal Farm*, I can tell right away if critics or cynics are bullshitting when they comment on *Think and Grow Rich* or *The Secret*, for that matter. Although often compared, the two books are very different. They're related, but they're different, which is why it's a dead giveaway when critics refer to them interchangeably.

Think and Grow Rich is a program of action. Organized planning comes up again and again in the book. And I mean organized planning *with a dollar amount attached to* it. Now, one of the things that Hill asks you to do in *Think and Grow Rich*, and it's vitally important, is that once you come up with your definite chief aim—and once you have distilled it into an exquisitely clear sentence that can be committed to paper in a plain and specific manner—you then must write down a dollar amount that you wish to earn in connection with your aim, the date by which you wish to earn it, and the services you will provide in exchange for this dollar amount.

Many people resist this step. I resisted it for years. People have different excuses and reasons for why they resist it. I resisted it because it seemed unspiritual, materialistic, and selfish. Other people resist it because setting a deadline by which to earn a certain sum of money seems far off or unrealistic. The second excuse is better than the first. There's never a good reason not to think of resources. Resources are the exchange of life.

We demonstrate who we are by where we spend. Time and money are the true resources that we're capable of giving to another person. Commerce is as vital a part of life as physicality. The Dead Sea Scrolls themselves are made up partly of contracts for an exchange of goods. Commerce goes back to our most primeval literature. It's a fact of life. Hence, you should drop all resistance to attaching a dollar amount and a date to your aim.

The amount can be a progressively earned sum. Almost certainly it's not going to come all at once. You can also select a date that is realistically pegged to the future, though not at so distant a point that it's easy to forget.

Do you recall that I was going to tell you about this sticky note that I was so glad I rediscovered in my copy of *Think and Grow Rich*? This was a sticky note that I had put in my personal copy of the book on my birthday of November 23, 2014. This was about a year after I had committed to reading the book with absolute dedication. On that day I wrote down a sum that I wanted to earn. And I wrote that I wanted to earn this sum by my birthday of the following year, November 23, 2015.

In terms of services, I wanted to write certain books that would bring me a very bold sum of money, which I personally wanted to earn one year to the day that I had written down this sum. I tucked away that copy of *Think and Grow Rich* and I actually forgot about having done this. It happened that I returned to that copy of the book on April 27, 2016, several months after I was supposed to have attained my financial goal, and I rediscovered my yellow sticky note. On the back of the note I wrote two words: "This happened!!"— with two exclamation points and the date. "This happened!!"

That was a powerful moment for me because I received a sum of money that was very close to what I had written down. And it was a bold figure. Not outlandish, but very bold. I received that sum of money by that date. I had forgotten about it, so when I came back to the book and found my sticky note I was excited, because it reflected the fruition of a step that I had long resisted.

Now, I think the reason why this is so important is that when you focus on a particular goal in your mind, and you're dead earnest about it, I do believe a few things are occurring. First, it is necessary and vital to not only provide a yardstick for oneself, but the mind, when it's really charged with emotion, functions as a kind of homing device. Almost like the cybernetic device that exists within a heat-seeking missile. It twists and turns, zigs and zags, but finally homes in on its target and moves toward it with efficiency and accuracy. I'm not saying that it's always going to happen with the exactitude that it happened to me; but I am saying, and I have evidence in my experience, that when you're emotionally charged with a certain aim, that's the time to be very serious and deadly earnest about numbers, dates, and deadlines.

You can't be shy about it. And remember, you're not broadcasting this experiment to others, more on which in a moment. This is yours; this is your aim. Hill emphasizes that you must commit your definite chief aim to paper; there's something very important about the tactile act of writing your aim on a sheet of paper, along with a sum of money and a date by which you intend to earn it— remember it could reach you progressively, not all at once—and the services you intend to provide in exchange for this sum.

Hill stresses that you must have the confidence, the faith, that you can actually reach your aim. Now, I have to admit that his insistence on faith has been a sticking point for me. What is faith? Defining it is almost like grasping at smoke. We all have different definitions. Some of us have none at all. I was told a story from a very reliable source who was present at the death vigil of a world-famous minister. I was told this in private, which is why I am not disclosing the minister's name. But, believe me, you'd recognize the name, and this was told to me by a family intimate. One of the minister's daughters came out of the room in which he was laying and said in despair: "Daddy has no faith."

I thought, what a heavy thing for the family member of a world-famous minister to say as he's laying on his deathbed. It puts you face-to-face with some things about yourself if you take that episode seriously. I don't know what faith is, but it occurred to me that anytime you encounter the term faith, if you have problems with it, as I do, you can substitute the word *persistence*, and you are very likely to home in on the same idea. Whenever I come upon the term faith in the work of Napoleon Hill I substitute persistence. Faith is expressed through persistence. So you don't have to concern yourself with subjective definitions of faith. I have none to offer you that hold water. But I feel that the expression of faith is persistence.

And there is something extraordinary in persistence. In as much as life makes this transcendent but tough bargain with us about a definite chief aim, a similar bargain is struck with us when we persist. Persistence is quite remarkable. It brings things to people that may have seemed impossible. I'm convinced that part of the reason for that is that it is a statistical law that runs of luck will always reverse, for the better or the worse. I've had the experience of seeing people who are really very mediocre succeed within their occupations. And it makes you wonder: how can a mediocre person succeed in a fairly competitive field? Part of the reason is persistence. If they're fortunate enough to have an indulgent boss, and they stick around for a while, they will unconsciously experience runs of luck that reverse one way or the other. And the fortunate reversals occur just often enough so that they survive. It's a peculiar feature of workplaces that successes are remembered much more than failures. This is why promotions are often not based on merit. Workplaces are generally not meritocracies. That fact can drive people to frustration. That's understandable. I remember once I was frustrated because a somewhat apathetic colleague got promoted about a year before I did. Sensing my frustration, a senior workmate took me aside and said: "Listen to me. Are you listening? This is not a meritocracy. Do you understand that? Repeat it, repeat it!" It was actually very helpful. Years later I understood the dynamic.

Remember: runs of luck reverse, and successes are remembered more than failures. Hence, people who are able to be persistent at a certain task, even if they are mediocre, do experience what might be called "dumb success." But this is not cause for despair. If you are effective, talented, and persistent, imagine how much more so this law can benefit you. Imagine how much more effective it can be if a truly capable person persists. In the long run, if someone who's really passionate, talented, and earnest about what he or she is doing is also persistent, the results can prove quite remarkable. Don't take it lightly. Be that person.

Chapter 5

The Power of the Master Mind

Once you have found your aim you don't have to share it with acquaintances and relatives. In fact, it's often best not to share it, because often other people will detract from or rundown your aim. That is a peculiarity of human nature: we lick our private wounds and dilute our regrets by running down other people's aims and wishes. It happens constantly. We've all had the experience: you sit next to Uncle Mike at Thanksgiving and he asks, what are you up to? You tell him you're trying to accomplish something, and he's got five different opinions about why that can't work. Even though the man has no experience, no background in what you're attempting. You don't need the opinions, peer pressure, or casual observations of other people. For now, you need only your most deeply felt conviction. There is a unique power in silence.

Napoleon Hill notes that most people, including relatives, friends, and coworkers, rush to offer you the cheapest commodity on Earth, which is an opinion. As a rule, they will be wrong about important things.

In *The Miracle of a Definite Chief Aim* I discuss cases where I've experienced real success, although I've had other people's opinions lined up against what I was doing. Rather than opinions you need *verifiable information*. You need expertise from people who warrant your trust. Sometimes you'll have to pay for that expertise, and it is well worth paying for. Sometimes that expertise will come for free, from what Napoleon Hill called a Master Mind group. The Master Mind group is where you exchange and share your innermost ideas in an atmosphere of comity, cooperation, and true willingness to help. You will need to look outside your group for business contacts, research, and specific professional advisement, but it is the nucleus of where you begin.

Hill capitalized the term Master Mind and I continue the practice here. The Master Mind is probably his most neglected step, because it involves doing things in an organized fashion with others. Most of us, myself included, like to think we're self-sufficient. But the Master Mind requires us to exit our comfort zone.

In short, a Master Mind is a collection of trusted, cooperative, similarly valued, and well-tempered people who meet on a regular basis, at least weekly, to mutually support one another's aims. The group can be as small as two people, but generally no larger than seven. Hill advised not surpassing seven members, but I have heard of successful Master Mind groups that number up to twelve.

Hill taught that this kind of trusting, harmonious group setting provides not only mutual trust, but also something greater. When two or more people gather for a shared purpose, he wrote, they are naturally pooling their mental energy, which produces the effect he called the Master Mind. Under this influence, he said, everyone's intuitions, insights, and intellectual acumen is heightened. In terms of his metaphysical beliefs, Hill reasoned that we live under Infinite Intelligence—Ralph Waldo Emerson called it the Over-soul—and that we're best able to tap Infinite Intelligence when we're functioning in a harmonious, cooperative group setting. This coalesces with Christ's dictum, "Where two or three gather in my name I am there with them." And this is also the spiritual basis behind the power people often experience in

Alcoholics Anonymous meetings. And there are other kinds of group meetings or congregational settings where people feel, I think quite rightly, that their enthusiasm, exuberance, energy, and insights are animated, lifted—mutually. There are certain things that we cannot do alone.

The intentional group is a profoundly valuable concept that was rediscovered as a tool of spiritual progress and self-development in the twentieth century. Spiritual philosopher G.I. Gurdjieff pioneered its use in the early twentieth century. Hill believed deeply in the agencies of a group meeting, and you can harness these agencies even amid just two people. And this is the setting—not among random people but among steady, trusted members—where you can share and exchange ideas, concerns, and needs.

I am part of a Master Mind group that meets Tuesday mornings at 11:30 eastern time. Its members are dispersed from Southern California to New England. We get together by conference call. We open each meeting by reading a set of Master Mind principles. I write about these principles and how to structure your meeting in a book called *The Power of the Master Mind*. We read the Master Mind principles, in which we dedicate ourselves to this covenant of mutual aid. Then each participant goes around and offers one piece of good news from the week past, and then each person discusses his or her wants and needs for the week ahead. We give advice, offer prayers, meditations, and listen to one another.

It's certainly not the only such form of collegiality that we have. We're out in the world consulting with collaborators, customers, professionals, and so forth. But, it is the area where everyone feels at liberty to stand exposed before one another and be very blunt and clear about one's aims and needs. That's the structured setting in which you can finally be completely transparent and honest. But there must be total trust and confidence in one another, and total harmony and cooperation. There can be no gossip or cliquishness within the group. There can be no politics. There must be a real spirit of earnest fellowship, similar to what you find in a 12-Step or Alcoholics Anonymous meeting. If you have that kind of setting among two or more people, you've got a Master Mind group. You should commit to meeting once a week. People's lives are messy—somebody gets sick, someone's away—but it should be a steady and reliable commitment.

As I've noted, it is tempting to neglect this step because it involves other people, because it requires setting aside time in a world where our time is a thinly stretched resource. But Hill insisted that the only way to gain access to what he called Infinite Intelligence, other than moments of sublime insight, is through the Master Mind group. By Infinite Intelligence he means a non-localized universal mind in which we all participate. He considered it the source of extrasensory insights and the overarching source of our own individual psyches. The Master Mind group is the irreplaceable means of contacting this higher mind. Hill talks elsewhere in the book about the exercise of convening an imaginary council of advisors—and that's entirely valid but he meant it as an adjunct to the Master Mind, not a substitute.

Again, here's the secret of *Think and Grow Rich*: Emotionalized thought directed toward one passionately held aim, aided by organized planning and *the Master Mind*, is the root of all accomplishment.

Through the Master Mind you become an inlet, as Hill saw it, for Infinite Intelligence. The Master Mind is Infinite Intelligence localized.

Chapter 6

Understanding Sex Transmutation

I'm now going to explore one fourth and final step. It is, in a sense, the taboo subject of *Think and Grow Rich*, one that people are often too embarrassed to talk about at business and motivational meetings. Napoleon Hill called it the "mystery of sex transmutation."

In 1960, one of my heroes, Earl Nightingale, a great radio broadcaster and motivational writer, produced and narrated an abridgment of *Think and Grow Rich*, something that I've also done. This being 1960, the publisher was too embarrassed or timorous to include sex transmutation as a topic, so Earl changed it to "enthusiasm," producing a vague and forgettable chapter. Hill, to his credit, took a great chance years earlier and included a highly innovative and insightful chapter on the topic in his signature book. And yet, nearly a generation later, Earl Nightingale, who I love, was too embarrassed to use that phraseology in his abridgement.

Now, I've met certain people in the alternative spiritual culture who regard *Think and Grow Rich* as an unserious book, a book for materially minded people, a book that's too adolescent—but sometimes such people will reverse themselves and say: "Wow, Hill's chapter on sex transmutation is one of the best things that's ever been written on the topic." Certain people who consider themselves chaos magicians or who are into ceremonial magick or psychological alchemy are actually working with sex transmutation—which I'll soon define—yet here you have the familiar-seeming figure of Napoleon Hill, who few such people regard as a radical or innovator, who wrote what is probably the clearest, most practical, most applicable, and broadly readable chapter on the topic.

Hill believed that the sexual impulse is actually the universal creative urge of life within men and women, and that the sexual impulse represents the urge of the individual not only to procreate and propagate the species, but to create *all things*. The great painter, the great artist, the great entrepreneur, the great businessperson, the great activist, the great diplomat—anyone who has something that they wish to concretize within the world—has, at their back, this drive of sexual expression. It often comes out only physically, but it's an expression of the overall creative principle of life seeking to actualize itself.

We see sex as something that's strictly physical because that's how we've been raised; but Hill is pointing out a higher truth that was gleaned by Vedic masters, Taoists, Kabbalists, practitioners of Tantra, and others today who are involved in chaos magick, ceremonial magick, and sex magick, all of which are interrelated. Over the course of time, this diffuse population of seekers has converged around the principle that the sexual urge is the life urge seeking expression. Again, this expression can be manifested through physicality, pleasure, and propagation of the species. Without it we wouldn't be here. But Hill taught that the sexual urge is at the back of everything that you as a generative being wish to create.

In the ancient Greek-Egyptian philosophy called Hermeticism we're told, "As above, so below." In Scripture we're told, "God created man in his own image." In these and other religious principles what we're really hearing, if you take them seriously, is that our birthright is generativity and productivity; we are to function as co-creators within our concentric sphere of existence. And the driving force behind this wish to produce, generate, and create is the sexual urge, of which procreation and pleasure are just one expression. But the other expressions appear in everything that the individual produces.

Hill gleaned this when very few modern people touched upon any such idea. Hill possessed this almost wild yet practical instinct for a topic that's deeply esoteric. He wrote about it very plainly. He made it into a practical formula. You can consciously harness the forces of sex transmutation, he wrote, by channeling the sexual urge *into some other form of creativity*. When you feel the sexual urge, rather than acting on it in the usual way, you redirect your thoughts toward the very thing you wish to create. In fact, he said that we're doing it all the time; that this is occurring whenever a salesman is demonstrating enthusiasm or personal magnetism; whenever an artist is exuding passion; whenever a minister is possessed by some kind of inspiration on the pulpit—that's the sexual urge being transmuted by thought into another channel of expression.

It is important to note that he's not prescribing celibacy. He's not saying that the sexual urge should be sublimated; in fact, he's very plain that a proper outlet for sexuality is therapeutic, healthy,

and necessary. But he does say that you can cultivate an awareness that sexuality is that raw urge
and energy that's behind everything that you want
to accomplish; and, you can at chosen moments
*redirect the sexual urge towards whatever creative
thing you want to out-picture in the world*; and that
you will then do so with greater energy, intellect,
and effectiveness.

This is interesting in light of our own era, in
which it is tempting to ask: Why do accomplished
people compromise their entire lives to satisfy the
sexual urge? I heard someone just the other day
at a dinner party asking this question. You see all
these powerful men, titans of politics, of media,
of culture, and they're brought down by the inap-
propriate pursuit of sex. People have asked, why?
Why would you sacrifice everything to engage in
an act of sex? I think it has something to do with
what Hill was getting at. Now, of course, there's
a lot of ego and a lot of other things caught up in
it, including entitlement, and so on. But for some
people it's a grossly misdirected use of this energy;
to some people it feels like life itself but it's mis-
construed. Hill specifically warned about this.
On one hand, this wild, frenzied energy can be
directed toward consensual pleasure, toward procreation, and toward productive things—without
it not only would the species not get propagated,

but bridges wouldn't get built, diseases wouldn't get cured, and beautiful works of art wouldn't get made. But if you permit that sexual urge to express itself only through physicality—or through an abusive physicality, where questions of consent and human respect are compromised—then this powerful principle gets corrupted.

Not surprisingly, sex transmutation is the most under-discussed topic in *Think and Grow Rich* because people find it embarrassing. They find it difficult to talk about. But what I'm describing is a faithful representation of what Hill was driving at—and it's a very productive principle. Certainly it has been helpful to me to identify some of the exuberance or enthusiasm that I feel towards my subject matter as something that is transmuted sexual energy. Hill even made the observation— and this may sound exaggerated—that if you can direct or transmute your sexual energy in the direction of something you wish to accomplish, you can be raised, at least temporarily, to the status of a genius. That language may seem far-flung— but I have to say that I have noticed in the lives of certain people this absolute drive that seems almost superhuman. And if they're not personally corrupt that drive can be a wonder to behold. Take, for example, the same friend who was raising this question of sexuality at the dinner party. At a

very young age he founded one of the most profitable and significant consulting companies in the
country. It's now a hugely successful consulting
company on a global scale. People have heard of
it. I remember a mutual acquaintance once saying
to me that my friend is almost like a figure from
another era, like a Benjamin Franklin, who seems
so possessed of energies that he appears almost
larger than life. That is an example of a kind of
unconscious sexual transmutation. If I talked to
him about any of this, he'd say, "You're out of your
mind!" But I think he's a perfect exemplar of this.

I have to say, frankly, and speaking from
personal experience, that I do bring a degree of
sexual transmutation to my work and my writing. People sometimes marvel at my work output
and ask, "How do you do it?" I do think some of
what Hill is describing is at the back of it. I feel
strongly this material should not be neglected.
It's very esoteric, it's very intriguing, and it's also
very practical. Hill did not spell it all out in min-
ute detail. You must personally experiment with
it. But I've given you a practical starting point.

I want to return to what I said at the beginning,
and what I've repeated several times because
it's vital. It is the secret to *Think and Grow Rich*,
which Hill says is encoded throughout the whole

book and appears several times in each chapter; it sometimes occurs to people on their first reading, and sometimes occurs to people only after they've read it multiple times. It is this, in my words, but faithful to the book:

Emotionalized thought directed toward one passionately held aim, aided by organized planning and the Master Mind, is the root of all accomplishment.

I believe I've shouted out the most important qualities of the book, which are:

1. Possessing a passionately felt and definite chief aim.

2. Engaging in organized planning, including committing to dates, dollar amounts, and services you intend to deliver.

3. Benefiting from the alliance of a Master Mind.

4. Using sex transmutation in pursuit of your aim.

Accompanying these steps is the power of emotionalized thought and persistence; the discipline to write down your clearly articulated aims and pursue them unceasingly; possessing an aim that fills you with passion so that procrastination has no place in your life; and avoiding errant opinions and seeking only sources of verifiable, valuable information.

These things, united, are the shared traits that Hill detected in notable and exceptional people from varying time periods and walks of life. One of the reasons *Think and Grow Rich* is so enduring, and this is true of *The Law of Success* as well, is that it is backed by a tremendous amount of journalistic research. Some of its language may feel antiquated. There's wild inconsistency in Hill's use of capitalizations and weird grammar and all kinds of peccadillos. And yet, the book stands up. It stands up because it was built on a foundation of great research and sweat equity. I believe that the secret to the book's posterity is that Hill dedicated the twenty years that he says he did to studying the common principles of success. If he didn't do that, the book would be one more piece of throwaway early-twentieth century motivational literature, of which there are mounds. This book lasted, because Hill's insights rested on authentic research.

I hope that this program has been profitable to you. I hope that it will drive you to return to *Think and Grow Rich*. If you've already read it, read it again, and read it again after that. If you've never read it, I hope this will serve as an introduction that moves you toward the book, and that within what I've written you will glean some idea of why it's vital to follow all of its steps, because they really coalesce into a magnificent whole.

My deepest wish for everyone experiencing this program is that you find real answers, real possibilities, and real self-development. And that these principles become practical pillars in your life. When they do, share them with others.

About the Author

Mitch Horowitz is a PEN Award-winning historian and the author of books including *Occult America; One Simple Idea: How Positive Thinking Reshaped Modern Life;* and *The Miracle Club: How Thoughts Become Reality.* A lecturer-in-residence at the University of Philosophical Research in Los Angeles, Mitch introduces and edits G&D Media's line of Condensed Classics and is the author of the Napoleon Hill Success Course series, including *The Miracle of a Definite Chief Aim, The Power of the Master Mind,* and *Secrets of Self-Mastery.* Visit him at MitchHorowitz.com.

Think and Grow Rich

Special Condensation

Chapter One
Desire
The First Step to Riches

In the early twentieth century a great American salesman and businessman named Edwin C. Barnes discovered how true it is that men really do *think and grow rich*.

Barnes's discovery did not come in one sitting. It came little by little, beginning with an ALL-CONSUMING DESIRE to become a business associate of inventor Thomas Edison. One of the chief characteristics of Barnes's desire was that it was *definite*. Barnes wanted to work *with* Edison—not just *for* him.

Straight off a freight train, Barnes presented himself in 1905 at Edison's New Jersey laboratory. He announced that he had come to go into business with the inventor. In speaking of their meeting years later, Edison said: "He stood there before me, looking like an ordinary tramp, but there was something in the expression of his face which conveyed the impression that he was determined to get what he had come after."

Barnes did *not* get his partnership with Edison on his first interview. But he *did* get a chance to work in the Edison offices, at a very nominal wage, doing a job that was unimportant to Edison—but *most important* to Barnes, because it gave him an opportunity to display his abilities to his future "partner."

Months passed. Nothing happened outwardly to bring Barnes any closer to his goal. But something important *was* happening in Barnes's mind. He was constantly intensifying his CHIEF DESIRE and his PLANS to become Edison's business associate.

Barnes was DETERMINED TO REMAIN READY UNTIL HE GOT THE OPPORTUNITY HE CAME FOR.

When the "big chance" arrived, it was in a different form, and from a different direction, than Barnes had expected. *That is one of the tricks of opportunity.* It has a sly habit of slipping in by the back door, and it often comes disguised as misfortune or temporary defeat. Perhaps this is why so many fail to wait for—or recognize—opportunity when it arrives.

Edison had just perfected a new device, known then as the Edison Dictating Machine. His salesmen were not enthusiastic. But Barnes saw his opportunity hidden in a strange-looking contraption that interested no one. Barnes seized the chance to sell the dictating machine, and did it so successfully that Edison gave him a contract to distribute and market it all over the world.

When Edwin C. Barnes climbed down from that freight train in Orange, New Jersey, he possessed one CONSUMING OBSESSION: to become the business associate of the great inventor. Barnes's desire was not a *hope!* It was not a *wish!* It was a keen, pulsating DESIRE, which transcended everything else. It was DEFINITE.

Wishing will not bring riches or other forms of success. But *desiring* riches with a state of mind that becomes an obsession, then planning definite ways and means to acquire riches, and backing those plans with persistence *that does not recognize failure*, will bring success.

The method by which DESIRE can be transmuted into its financial equivalent, consists of six definite, practical steps.

FIRST

Fix in your mind the *exact* amount of money you desire. It is not sufficient merely to say, "I want plenty of money." Be definite as to the amount.

SECOND

Determine exactly what you intend to give in return for the money you desire.

THIRD

Establish a definite date when you intend to *possess* the money you desire.

FOURTH

Create *a definite plan* for carrying out your desire, and begin *at once*, whether or not you are ready, to put this plan into *action*.

FIFTH

Write out a clear, concise statement of the amount of money you intend to acquire, name the time limit for its acquisition, state what you intend to give in return for the money, and describe clearly the plan through which you intend to accumulate it.

SIXTH

Read your written statement aloud, twice daily, once just before retiring at night and once after arising in

the morning. AS YOU READ—SEE AND FEEL AND
BELIEVE YOURSELF ALREADY IN POSSESSION
OF THE MONEY.

It is especially important that you observe and follow number six. You may complain that it is impossible for you to "see yourself in possession of money"
before you actually have it. Here is where a BURN-
ING DESIRE will come to your aid. If you truly
DESIRE money or another goal so keenly that your
desire is an obsession, you will have no difficulty
in convincing yourself that you will acquire it. The
object is to want it so much and become so determined that you CONVINCE yourself you will have
it. In future chapters you will learn why this is so
important.

Chapter Two
Faith
The Second Step to Riches

FAITH is the head chemist of the mind. When FAITH
is blended with the vibration of thought, the subconscious mind instantly picks up the vibration, trans-
lates it into its spiritual equivalent, and transmits it to
Infinite Intelligence, as in the case of prayer.

ALL THOUGHTS THAT HAVE BEEN EMO-
TIONALIZED (given feeling) AND MIXED WITH
FAITH begin immediately to translate themselves
into their physical equivalent.

If you have difficulty getting a grasp of just what
faith is, think of it as a special form of *persistence*—one
that we feel when we *know* that we have right at our
backs and that helps us persevere through setbacks
and temporary failure.

To develop this quality in yourself, use this five-
step formula. Promise yourself to read, repeat, and
abide by these steps—and write down your promise.

FIRST
I know that I have the ability to achieve the object of
my DEFINITE PURPOSE in life, therefore, I *demand*
of myself persistent, continuous action toward its
attainment, and I here and now promise to render
such action.

SECOND
I realize the dominating thoughts of my mind will
eventually reproduce themselves in outward physical
action, and gradually transform themselves into physical reality. Therefore, I will concentrate my thoughts
for thirty minutes daily upon the task of thinking of
the person I intend to become, thereby creating in my
mind a clear mental picture of that person.

THIRD

I know that through the principle of auto suggestion any desire that I persistently hold in my mind will eventually seek expression through some practical means of attaining the object back of it. Therefore, I will devote ten minutes daily to demanding of myself the development of *self-confidence.*

FOURTH

I have clearly written down a description of my DEFINITE CHIEF AIM in life, and I will never stop trying until I have developed sufficient self-confidence for its attainment.

FIFTH

I fully realize that no wealth or position can long endure unless built upon truth and justice. Therefore, I will engage in no transaction which does not benefit all whom it affects. I will succeed by attracting to myself the forces I wish to use, and the cooperation of other people. I will induce others to serve me, because of my willingness to serve others. I will eliminate hatred, envy, jealousy, selfishness, and cynicism, by developing love for all humanity, because I know that a negative attitude toward others can never bring me success. I will cause others to believe in me because I will believe in them, and in myself.

I will sign my name to this formula, commit it to memory, and repeat it aloud once a day, with full FAITH that it will gradually influence my THOUGHTS and ACTIONS, so that I will become a self-reliant and successful person.

Chapter Three
Auto Suggestion
The Third Step to Riches

AUTO SUGGESTION is a term that applies to all suggestions and self-administered stimuli that reach one's mind through the five senses. Stated another way: *auto suggestion is self suggestion.*

It is the agency of communication between the conscious and subconscious minds. But your subconscious mind recognizes and acts ONLY upon thoughts that have been well mixed with *emotion or feeling.* This is a fact of such importance as to warrant repetition.

When you begin to use—and keep using—the three-step program for auto suggestion in this chapter, be on the alert for hunches from your subconscious mind—and when they appear, put them into ACTION IMMEDIATELY.

FIRST

Go into some quiet spot (preferably in bed at night) where you will not be disturbed or interrupted, close your eyes, and repeat aloud (so you may hear your own words) the written statement of the amount of money you intend to accumulate, the time limit for its accumulation, and a description of the service or merchandise you intend to give in return for the money. As you carry out these instructions SEE YOURSELF ALREADY IN POSSESSION OF THE MONEY.

For example: Suppose that you intend to accumulate $50,000 by the first of January, five years hence, and that you intend to give personal services in return for the money in the capacity of a salesman. Your written statement of your purpose should be similar to the following:

"By the first day of January, I will have in my possession $50,000, which will come to me in various amounts from time to time during the interim.

"In return for this money I will give the most efficient service of which I am capable, rendering the fullest possible quantity and the best possible quality of service in the capacity of salesman of . . . (and describe the service or merchandise you intend to sell).

"I believe that I will have this money in my possession. My faith is so strong that I can now see this money before my eyes. I can touch it with my hands. It is now awaiting transfer to me at the time and in the proportion that I deliver the service I intend to render for it. I am awaiting a plan by which to accumulate this money, and I will follow that plan when it is received."

SECOND
Repeat this program night and morning until you can see (in your imagination) the money you intend to accumulate.

THIRD
Place a written copy of your statement where you can see it night and morning, and read it just before retiring and upon arising, until it has been memorized.

Chapter Four
Specialized Knowledge
The Fourth Step to Riches

General knowledge, no matter how great in quantity or variety, is of little use in accumulating money. Knowledge is only *potential* power. It becomes power only when, and if, it is organized into *definite plans of action,* and directed toward a *definite end.*

In connection with your aim, you must decide what sort of specialized knowledge you require, and the purpose for which it is needed. To a large extent, your major purpose in life, and the goal toward which you are working, will help determine what knowledge you need. With this question settled, your next move requires that you have ACCURATE INFORMATION concerning DEPENDABLE SOURCES OF KNOWL- EDGE.

Look toward many high-quality sources for the knowledge you seek: people, courses, partnerships, books—look everywhere. Some of this knowledge will be free—never undervalue what is free—and some will require purchasing. Decide what knowledge you seek—and pursue it completely. The author spent more than twenty years interviewing people and studying success methods before writing this book.

Without specialized knowledge, your ideas remain mere wishes. Once you have acquired the knowledge you need, you can use your critical faculty of *imagination* to combine your IDEAS with this SPECIALIZED KNOWLEDGE, and make ORGANIZED PLANS to carry out your aims.

This is the formula for capability: *Using imagination to combine specialized knowledge with ideas and to form organized plans.*

The connecting ingredient is imagination, which we will now learn to cultivate.

Chapter Five

Imagination
The Fifth Step to Riches

The imagination is the workshop wherein are fashioned all plans created by man. The impulse, the DESIRE, is literally given shape, form, and ACTION through the aid of the imaginative faculty of the mind.

Through the medium of creative imagination, the finite mind of man has direct communication with Infinite Intelligence. Imagination is the faculty through which "hunches" and "inspirations" are reached. It is by this faculty that all basic or new ideas are handed over to man. It is through this faculty that thought vibrations from the minds of others are received. It is through this faculty that one individual may "tune in" or communicate with the subconscious minds of others.

The creative imagination works only when the conscious mind is stimulated through the emotion of a STRONG DESIRE. This is highly significant.

What's more, the creative faculty may have become weak through inaction. Your imagination becomes more alert and more receptive in proportion to its development through *use*.

After you have completed this book, return to this section and begin at once to put your imagination to work on the building of a plan, or plans, for the transmutation of *desire* into money, or your core aim. Reduce your plan to writing. The moment you complete this, you will have *definitely* given concrete form to the intangible *desire*.

This step is extremely important. When you reduce the statement of your desire, and a plan for its realization, into writing, you have actually *taken the first* of a series of steps that will enable you to covert your *thought* into its physical counterpart.

Chapter Six
Organized Planning
The Sixth Step to Riches

It is vital that you form a DEFINITE, practical plan, or plans, to carry out your aims. You will now learn how to build plans that are *practical*, as follows:

FIRST
Ally yourself with a group of as many people as you may need for the creation and carrying out of your plan or plans for the accumulation of money—making

use of the "Master Mind" principle described in a later chapter. (Compliance with this instruction is essential. Do not neglect it.)

SECOND

Before forming your "Master Mind" alliance, decide what advantages and benefits you may offer the individual members of your group in return for their cooperation. No one will work indefinitely without some form of compensation. No intelligent person will either request or expect another to work without adequate compensation, although this may not always be in the form of money.

THIRD

Arrange to meet with the members of your "Master Mind" group at least twice a week, and more often if possible, until you have jointly perfected the necessary plan or plans for the accumulation of money.

FOURTH

Maintain *perfect harmony* between yourself and every member of your "Master Mind" group. If you fail to carry out this instruction to the letter, you may expect to meet with failure. The "Master Mind" principle *cannot* obtain where *perfect harmony* does not prevail.

Keep in mind these facts:

1. You are engaged in an undertaking of major importance to you. To be sure of success, you must have plans that are faultless.

2. You must have the advantage of the experience, education, native ability, and imagination of other minds. This is in harmony with the methods followed by every person who has accumulated a great fortune.

Now, if the first plan you devise does not work successfully, replace it with a new plan. If this new plan fails to work, replace it, in turn, with still another, and so on, until you find a plan that *does work*. Right here is the point where the majority of men meet with failure, because of their lack of *persistence* in creating new plans to take the place of those that fail.

Remember this when your plans fail: *Temporary defeat is not permanent failure.*

No follower of this philosophy can reasonably expect to accumulate a fortune without experiencing "temporary defeat." When defeat comes, accept it as a signal that your plans are not sound, rebuild those plans, and set sail once more toward your goal.

Finally, as you are devising your plans keep in mind these Major Attributes of Leadership—traits possessed by the greatest achievers:

1. Unwavering Courage
2. Self-Control
3. A Keen Sense of Justice
4. Definiteness of Decision
5. Definiteness of Plans
6. The Habit of Doing More Than Paid For
7. A Pleasing Personality
8. Sympathy and Understanding
9. Mastery of Detail
10. Willingness to Assume Full Responsibility
11. Cooperation With Others

Chapter Seven
Decision
The Seventh Step to Riches

Analysis of several hundred people who had accumulated fortunes disclosed that *every one of them* had the habit of *reaching decisions promptly*, and of changing these decisions slowly, if and when they were changed. People who fail to accumulate money, *without exception*, have the habit of reaching decisions, if at all, very *slowly*, and of *changing these decisions quickly and often*.

What's more, the majority of people who fail to accumulate money sufficient for their needs tend to be easily influenced by the "opinions" of others. "Opinions" are the cheapest commodities on earth. Everyone has a flock of opinions ready to be wished upon anyone who will accept them. If you are influenced by "opinions" when you reach *decisions*, you will not succeed in any undertaking, much less in that of transmuting *your own desire* into money.

If you are influenced by the opinions of others, you will have no DESIRE of your own.

Keep your own counsel when you begin to put into practice the principles described here by *reaching your own decisions* and following them. Take no one into your confidence *except* the members of your "Master Mind" group, and be very sure in your selection of this group that you choose ONLY those who will be in COMPLETE SYMPATHY AND HARMONY WITH YOUR PURPOSE.

Close friends and relatives, while not meaning to, often handicap one through "opinions" and sometimes through ridicule, which is meant to be humorous. Thousands of men and women carry inferiority complexes with them throughout life, because some well-meaning but ignorant person destroyed their confidence through "opinions" or ridicule.

You have a mind of your own. USE IT and reach your own decisions. If you need facts or information from others to enable you to reach decisions, as you probably will in many instances, acquire these facts or secure the information you need quietly, without disclosing your purpose.

Those who reach DECISIONS promptly and definitely know what they want and generally get it. Leaders in every walk of life DECIDE quickly and firmly. That is the major reason why they are leaders. The world has a habit of making room for the man whose words and actions show that he knows where he is going.

Chapter Eight
Persistence
The Eighth Step to Riches

PERSITENCE is an essential factor in transmuting DESIRE into its monetary equivalent. The basis of persistence is the POWER OF WILL.

Will power and desire, when properly combined, make an irresistible pair. Men who accumulate great fortunes are generally known as cold-blooded and sometimes ruthless. Often they are misunderstood. What they have is will power, which they mix with persistence, and place at the back of their desires to *ensure* the attainment of their objectives.

Lack of persistence is one of the major causes of failure. Experience with thousands of people has proved that lack of persistence is a weakness common to the majority of men. It is a weakness that may be overcome by effort. The ease with which lack of persistence may be conquered depends *entirely* upon the INTENSITY OF ONE'S DESIRE.

In short, THERE IS NO SUBSTITUTE FOR PERSISTENCE! It cannot be supplanted by any other quality! Remember this and it will hearten you in the beginning when the going may seem difficult and slow.

Those who have cultivated the HABIT of persistence seem to enjoy insurance against failure. No matter how many times they are defeated, they finally arrive toward the top of the ladder. Sometimes it appears that there is a hidden Guide whose duty is to test men through all sorts of discouraging experiences. Those who pick themselves up after defeat and keep on trying arrive at their destination. The hidden Guide lets no one enjoy great achievement without passing the PERSISTENCE TEST.

What we DO NOT SEE, what most of us never suspect of existing, is the silent but irresistible POWER that comes to the rescue of those who fight on in the face of discouragement. If we speak of this power at all, we call it PERSISTENCE.

There are four simple steps that lead to the habit of PERSISTENCE.

1. A definite purpose backed by burning desire for its fulfillment.

2. A definite plan, expressed in continuous action.
3. A mind closed tightly against all negative and discouraging influences, including negative suggestions of relatives, friends, and acquaintances.
4. A friendly alliance with one or more persons who will encourage you to follow through with both plan and purpose.

Chapter Nine
The Master Mind
The Ninth Step to Riches

The "Master Mind" may be defined as: "Coordination of knowledge and effort, in a spirit of harmony, between two or more people for the attainment of a definite purpose."

No individual may hold great power without availing himself of the "Master Mind." A previous chapter supplied instructions for the creation of PLANS for the purpose of translating DESIRE into its monetary equivalent. If you carry out these instructions with PERSISTENCE and intelligence, and use discrimination in selecting your "Master Mind" group, your objective will have been halfway reached, even before you begin to recognize it.

The Master Mind brings an obvious economic advantage, by allowing you to surround yourself with the advice, counsel, and personal cooperation of a group of people who are willing to lend you whole-hearted aid in a spirit of PERFECT HARMONY. But there is also a more abstract phase; it may be called the PSYCHIC PHASE.

The psychic phase of the Master Mind is more difficult to comprehend because it has reference to the spiritual forces with which the human race, as a whole, is not well acquainted. You may catch a significant suggestion from this statement: "No two minds ever come together without, thereby, creating a third invisible, intangible force which may be likened to a third mind."

The human mind is a form of energy, a part of it being spiritual in nature. When the minds of two people are coordinated in a SPIRIT OF HARMONY the spiritual units of energy of each mind form an affinity, which constitutes the "psychic" phase of the Master Mind.

Analyze the record of any man who has accumulated a great fortune, and many of those who have accumulated modest fortunes, and you will find that they have either consciously or unconsciously employed the "Master Mind."

Great power can be accumulated through no other principle!

Chapter Ten
Sex Transmutation
The Tenth Step to Riches

The meaning of the word "transmute" is, in simple language, "the changing or transferring of one element, or form of energy, into another." The emotion of sex brings into being a unique and powerful state of mind that can be used for extraordinary intellectual and material creative purposes.

This is accomplished through *sex transmutation*, which means the switching of the mind from thoughts of physical expression to thoughts of some other nature.

Sex is the most powerful of human desires. When driven by this desire, men develop keenness of imagination, courage, will power, persistence, and creative ability unknown to them at other times. So strong and impelling is the desire for sexual contact that men freely run the risk of life and reputation to indulge it.

When harnessed and redirected along other lines, this motivating force maintains all of its attributes of keenness of imagination, courage, etc., which may be used as powerful creative forces in literature, art, or in any other profession or calling, including, of course, the accumulation of riches.

The transmutation of sex energy calls for the exercise of will power, to be sure, but the reward is worth the effort. The desire for sexual expression is inborn and natural. The desire cannot, and should not, be submerged or eliminated. But it should be given an outlet through forms of expression that enrich the body, mind, and spirit. If not given this form of outlet, through transmutation, it will seek outlets through purely physical channels.

The emotion of sex is an "irresistible force." When driven by this emotion, men become gifted with a super power for action. Understand this truth, and you will catch the significance of the statement that sex transmutation will lift one into the status of a genius. The emotion of sex contains the secret of creative ability.

When harnessed and transmuted, this driving force is capable of lifting men to that higher sphere of thought which enables them to master the sources of worry and petty annoyance that beset their pathway on the lower plane.

The major reason why the majority of men who succeed do not begin to do so until after the ages of forty to fifty (or beyond), is their tendency to DISSAPTE their energies through over indulgence in physical expression of the emotion of sex. The majority of men *never* learn that the urge of sex has other possibilities, which far transcend in importance that of mere physical expression.

But remember, sexual energy must be *transmuted* from desire for physical contact into some *other* form of desire and action, in order to lift one to the status of a genius.

Chapter Eleven
The Subconscious Mind
The Eleventh Step to Riches

The subconscious mind is the connecting link between the finite mind of man and Infinite Intelligence. It is the intermediary through which one may draw upon the forces of Infinite Intelligence at will. It alone contains the secret process by which mental impulses are modified and changed into their spiritual equivalent. It alone is the medium through which prayer may be transmitted to the source capable of answering prayer.

I never approach the discussion of the subconscious mind without a feeling of littleness and inferiority due, perhaps, to the fact that man's entire stock of knowledge on the subject is so pitifully limited. The very fact that the subconscious mind is the medium of communication between the thinking mind of man and Infinite Intelligence is, of itself, a thought that almost paralyzes one's reason.

After you have accepted as a reality the existence of your subconscious mind, and understand its possibilities for transmuting your DESIRES into their physical or monetary equivalent, you will understand why you have been repeatedly urged to MAKE YOUR DESIRES CLEAR, AND TO REDUCE THEM TO WRITING. You will also understand the necessity of PERSISTENCE in carrying out instructions.

The thirteen principles in this book are the stimuli with which—through practice and persistence—you acquire the ability to reach and influence your subconscious mind.

Chapter Twelve
The Brain
The Twelfth Step to Riches

More than twenty years before writing this book, the author, working with the late Dr. Alexander Graham Bell and Dr. Elmer R. Gates, observed that every human brain is both a broadcasting and receiving station for the vibration of thought.

The Creative Imagination is the "receiving set" of the brain, which receives thoughts released by the brains of others. It is the agency of communication between one's conscious, or reasoning, mind, and the outer sources from which one may receive thought stimuli.

When stimulated, or "stepped up," to a high rate of vibration, the mind becomes more receptive to the vibration of thought from outside sources. This "stepping up" occurs through the positive emotions or the negative emotions. Through the emotions the vibrations of thought may be increased. This is why it is crucial that your goal have strong emotions at the back of it.

Vibrations of an exceedingly high rate are the only vibrations picked up and carried from one brain to another. Thought is energy travelling at an exceedingly high rate of vibration. Thought that has been modified or "stepped up" by any of the major emotions vibrates at a much higher rate than ordinary thought, and it is this type of thought that passes from one mind to another, through the broadcasting machinery of the human brain.

Thus, you will see that the broadcasting principle is the factor through which you mix feeling or emotion with your thoughts and pass them on to your subconscious mind, or to the minds of others.

Chapter Thirteen
The Sixth Sense
The Thirteenth Step to Riches

The thirteenth and final principle is known as the "sixth sense," through which Infinite Intelligence may and will communicate voluntarily, without any effort or demands by the individual.

After you have mastered the principles in this book, you will be prepared to accept as true a statement that may otherwise seem incredible, namely: Through the aid of the sixth sense you will be warned of impending dangers in time to avoid them, and notified of opportunities in time to embrace them.

With the development of the sixth sense, there comes to your aid, and to do your bidding, a kind of "guardian angel" who will open to you at all times the door to the Temple of Wisdom.

Whether this is a statement of truth, you will never know except by following the instructions described in this book, or some similar method.

The author is not a believer in, nor an advocate of, "miracles," for the reason that he has enough knowledge of Nature to understand that Nature *never deviates from her established laws.* Some of her laws are so incomprehensible that they produce what appear to be "miracles."

The sixth sense comes as near to being a miracle as anything I have ever experienced.

Epilogue
A Word About Fear

As you begin any new undertaking you are likely at one point or another to find yourself gripped by the emotion of fear.

Fear should never be bargained with or capitulated to. It takes the charm from one's personality, destroys the possibility of accurate thinking, diverts concentration of effort, masters persistence, turns the will power into nothingness, destroys ambition, beclouds the memory, and invites failure in every conceivable form. It kills love, assassinates the finer emotions of the heart, discourages friendship, and leads to sleeplessness, misery, and unhappiness.

So pernicious and destructive is the emotion of fear that it is, almost literally, worse than anything that can befall you.

If you suffer from a fear of poverty, reach a decision to get along with whatever wealth you can accumulate WITHOUT WORRY. If you fear the loss of love, reach a decision to get along without love, if that is necessary. If you experience a general sense of worry, reach a blanket decision that *nothing* life has to offer is *worth* the price of worry.

And remember: The greatest of all remedies for fear is a BURNING DESIRE FOR ACHIEVEMENT, backed by useful service to others.

Printed in the USA
CPSIA information can be obtained
at www.ICGtesting.com
JSHW011416160824
R13664500002B/R136645PG68134JSX00025B/1